Prison Segmentation for Defense Support Teams

Can Better Info Help?

Rev. Mike Wanner

Copyright
Rev. Mike Wanner
February 8, 2018

Selected Images Used by License

Table of Contents

Table of Contents 3
Introduction 4
1 - Disclaimer 5
2 - Why I am Writing This Book 6
3 - Let's Create Pre-Plea Input Options 7
4 - Information Can Be Power 8
5 - Cost Neutral Options Critical? 9
6 - How Can A Prisoner Help 10
7 - Routine Delay Possibility 11
8 - Booking Categories 13
9 - The Comprehensive Detainee Story 14
10 - Employed & Unemployed Detainees 16
11 - Universal Employer Calls 18
12 - Categories of Detainees 19
13 - Substance Abuse Detainees 20
14 - Mental Health Detainees 21
15 - One Day Delay Startup 22
16 - Diagnostic Evaluations 24
17 - Cost Savings Could be Tremendous 25
18 - Quality Of Life Expansion Factors 26
19 - Two or More Day Delays 27
20 - Payback by Saving A Child From Crisis 28
21 - The Good Defense Support Teams Can Do 29
22 - Optional Idea 30
23 - Thank You 31
24 - Don't Worry Ever 32
25 - Resource List 33
26 - Angels Please Prayers 35
27 - Private Channeling 36
28 - Reverend Mike Wanner 38

Introduction

It is Super Bowl Parade day in Philadelphia, and the Angel of Healing is once again planting a title seed in my head before I get up. Once again, I am saying "Really" as I have not yet realized the depth of the idea.

Eagles fans are celebrating all over Philadelphia as the Eagles won Super Bowl VII but I will be home writing, and that is all as it should be.

One of the complications in our system of jurisprudence is representation for those with limited resources. This can be a vulnerability for those individuals but also for all citizens everywhere because as expenses rise, it can become more difficult for the court to provide alternative paths for those who could benefit from the optional processes if the right time and information could be assembled.

We do not have a shortage of convicted citizens, and we are not really in need of more unless they are entirely deserving of the loss of freedom. Let us all help defend the security of the system and finances of our country and also try to help convicted prisoners to limit the addition of more to their number.

Let's talk about offering prisoners the opportunity to help arrested persons pre-trial to document their situation and make a case for avoiding incarceration when possible. In the meantime, successful prisoner negotiators could develop skills and friends for their later Reentry.

1 - Disclaimer

I, the author, am not involved with prisons or prisoners but I have talked to many prisoners during Hospital Pastoral Visitations. I am sharing what is coming to me in an effort to spread understanding and trigger conversations that can be helpful. It may be that the discussion needs finessing and I invite your wisdom into the mix.

My guidance has suggested that a lot can be done to strengthen the system for all users. I will detail my views which are not the expert positions of a Lawyer or Law clerk or Corrections Officer or Corrections Administrator or Corrections Manager or Corrections Supervisor, or Medical Practitioner or Psychologist or Psychiatrist or Social Worker or another expert who might be helpful here.

As I have said many times before, everything that I look at about prisons seems to be so complicated. Here I suggest some things that have come to my awareness regarding the early stages of the system.

2 - Why I am Writing This Book

Every day is new, and we need the new possibilities that did not exist the previous day. Let's talk about a preplan, communication and structure to reshape flows with more freedom, more security, and less risk.

Let us help develop a new working plan. All of this takes time so let's consider steps that allow a lot more independence. I hope that you can find options that bring peace, security, and flow.

This book is intended as a conversation starter because the rigidity of thinking needs to be redirected to more benefits at minimal risk for the whole system. The right resources at the right place at the right time can maximize safety for prison staff and prisoners while being economical for the bill payers we know as taxpayers.

3 - Let's Create Pre-Plea Input Options

Public defenders are very busy, and it may be that they are not able to explain as much as they would like to their clients. Time can move fast, and defendants could be overwhelmed by their situation and the choices they have to make.

While defendants have rights, they may lack understanding, and they may be their own worst enemy. Let's us consider a system whereby arraignment could be slowed a bit by having some path options for those arrested.

4 - Information Can Be Power

When people find themselves in a new situation, it is not unusual for people to look for guidance from others who have been there before. Persons arrested are limited to who they can talk to, and it is very likely that many of the people in that category are probably not much better informed.

It is likely impossible to guess what information might be available to everybody in that situation, Depending upon the authorities processing protocols in various jurisdictions,

Arrested persons may have no idea of the details that could work against them:

1. Evidence.

2. Size of a worst possible sentence of what is normal.

3. Their chances at a trial

4. A prosecutor will make an offer.

5. What options the defense suggests.

6. The lack of possibility for options.

7. Anything they can do to prepare.

5 - Cost Neutral Options Critical?

Prisoners have walked in the shoes of those recently arrested and being in jail may help them to be motivated to keep others out. Also, assisting others could support them as they try to get their lives back together.

Jobs on the outside will still likely be an issue so why not create new options that can improve or shorten a prisoner's sentence, enhance the quality of their current sentence, have them make some friends and improve the prospects for those entering the jurisprudence system in the region.

Benefits to justify the system may have many results. The obvious is:

1. Maximize the choices available to the arrested.

2. The potential to find information that will identify rights that may not be obvious.

3. Optimizing the time available for the skills of the designated defender.

4. Time for comprehensive analysis.

5. Prisoners skills identification for potential later employment in the legal system.

6. Keeping as many people out of prison as can be justified.

6 - How Can A Prisoner Help

Options can vary depending on the laws and rules of different courts throughout the land. The concept here is about coming from nothing and creating an initiative that might help the whole system.

Every prisoner has walked in the shoes of those who are in a pre-plea situation. The crisis of confusion and the need for clarity may be enough to help some detainees to be open to wise advice.

The idea here is an impartial resource to help destress the pre-plea time for the detainees by allowing them to converse with someone who has been there. The role of the prisoner would not be one of a legal advisor but one of a de-stressor and information gatherer.

The recommendation would be for a prisoner in segmentation to reflect on their experience and draft some ideas to generate options. Forms, computer programs, restricted telephone calls could all be part of the situation and could vary by facility, state, and type of government agency in charge of the institution and staff of each facility.

A prisoner in segmentation could be able to work on this or better might be a team of prisoners in segmentation who could all work together to create Options.

7 - Routine Delay Possibility

The time criticality of arraignment and the importance of the plea set many things in motion that may have long-reaching effects. Everything that is in place makes some sense and may have been more reasonable in the past than it is now.

The things decided under stress may not be optimal for the arrested person yet the decision may impact their life for years to come. It could be essential to make progress on all this in a very incremental way.

Early steps would involve an introduction to the plea process. This could be done in different formats, and those that follow are only a partial list of ideas that prisoners may want to include in their offerings:

1. Intro Whitepaper

2. Critical Info Alert and extended stay info.

3. Identification that early conversations are with prisoners and not their defenders.

4. Audio introduction or Video introduction

5. Personal History-Info Form for Defender.

6. Career Impact Advisory

7. Rights to Legal Representation

8. Rights to Legal Representation for Those with Limited Means.

9. What to prepare before you meet a public defender.

10. Why a detainee should get to work and think about their options.

11. Option resource information that may be available locally.

12. Clear and direct materials from the courts that clearly lay out processes and potential consequences.

Routine delays would need to be offered freely by prisoners, but in the interest of security, there should be a couple of ideas considered by the administration.

Things to consider:

1. Prisoners and detainee identities should not be known to each other. An ID code of some kind might be helpful to allow appreciation gifts/contributions to the prisoner.

2. Detainees should be allowed to request a routine delay helper to assist them further.

3. Detainees may be allowed to make some phone calls to their children and parents to soften the impact.

4. Detainees may be allowed to do employer outreach.

5. Detainee Personal Information security.

8 - Booking Categories

Efficiency can come through sorting of services needed and minimizing one size fits all protocols. In mass casualty situations, there is a protocol for sorting which comes from the French word "Triage."

Triage for patients gets them moving on the right path to the services that are needed more expediently. Sorting arrested persons may streamline processing and cuts costs.

Persons arrested for the white-collar crimes and those with addiction issues may in some jurisdictions go through the exact same processes. Legal Waivers could help to allow healthy white-collar criminals out of the queue for the doctor and let them get to work on a report for their legal representative.

In jurisprudence like everything else, time is money. Having fewer people going to see professionals can save costs and time.

The drug addict booked behind the white-collar criminal may need the doctor more imminently. Delayed care for any reason can cause lawsuits.

Prison systems seem to be very complicated and strictly run. There is sound reasoning behind that diligence and getting creative without permission can cost staff their jobs so they may not be prone to do that.

Creative systems with permissions can change the density, intensity, sustainability, flexibility, and costs of the system. Let's get creative with permission.

9 - The Comprehensive Detainee Story

The success of this program could be significantly influenced by the comprehensiveness of the defense support teams' documentation. Whether the representation is compensated or not, the developed complete detainee story can make a huge difference in the number of people who are incarcerated.

There could be many minute details that could be captured and used by the defense team to frame the humanity of the detainee as possibilities for unique consideration. Detail accumulation takes time, and a rush to establish a plea may not be to anyone's advantage.

It, of course, will vary by jurisdiction, but objective persons may be concerned that the standard practice applied as default circumstances may evolve to be more automatic than diligent. Each person is unique, and it is essential that the system represents that uniqueness so that any errors that occur are on the side of reasonably acceptable margins of a not-guilty verdict instead of a conviction.

There are two presenters of the evidence and witnesses before a court of law. The prosecutors are paid staff persons of the government who have all the time they need to prepare and present a case.

The defense may not be as well supported, or some may be entirely "Pro Bono," and that could in some cases equate to somewhat of an actual disadvantage for any detainee. Defense counsel who is time-crunched may be less able to prepare a highly comprehensive presentation.

Even detainees with well-compensated representation need to be ready for presentation of any justification for the behavior that was witnessed by the authorities or witnesses.

Physical, Emotional, Mental and Spiritual circumstances can all contribute to the stress, anxiety and mental alertness state of detainees at the time they were detained.

Taking the time to create a comprehensive story for each detainee can help to develop options in the short and long term. Ideally, detailed stories can promote understanding and may provide enough information for further development of the defense support team concept.

10 - Employed & Unemployed Detainees

When I thought about this heading, my initial reaction was that it is discriminatory. WOW was my next thought; I am thoroughly against bias so I should not be writing that.

Well, I am also against throwing out the baby with the bathwater. It is not discriminatory to anybody to try to use resources wisely so the optimal value will be delivered to all with the dollars available.

Employed persons who earn an income usually use that income to support their families. No paycheck equals no support equals more support claims to government programs which equals more taxes and higher costs for everybody.

Common Sense is my friend, so I will include this chapter and apologize to all who are offended. We collectively need to defend the taxpayers as best we can.

Detainees with a little consideration may be able to contact their employers, so the employer is not left high and dry and uninformed. Employers who are ignored can be damaged by employees' non-performance as scheduled and can easily reject untimely excuses and be less than cooperative with benefits.

Arrested for a simple indiscretion which may later be voided can accidentally ruin a persons' career and jeopardize the quality of life for their family. People who are hurt this way can be vengeful and retaliatory.

The time saved in streamlined categorization as in Chapter 8 may be just enough to allow an employee to give his employer a heads up and keep the relationship and their standing.

Unemployed detainees should not experience a detriment because an employed person was allowed some leeway. They could actually be benefitted by the rethinking of the system processes.

Prisoners who embark on the prison segmentation project should be aware of this issue and build some similar benefits into their proposals for each category member.

The taxpayers could easily favor some accommodation for employed detainees because accommodating them could lead to many system benefits like:

1. Possibility for Work Release instead of Incarceration

2. Detainee's families being supported by employee benefits and not state welfare programs.

3. Treatment programs funded by employers instead of taxpayers.

4. Stable business activity for employers.

5. Low or minimal Incarceration.

6. Less Recidivism

7. Detainees are paying for part of their delay days.

11 - Universal Employer Calls

While I explained above the reasons to bring in employers and this may seem redundant, I add this section because the employability of all detainees is critical to the economic balance of the whole incarceration rehabilitation effort that can save families and communities.

While an employed person may do some less than wise things that bring them to the attention of law enforcement, it is critical that the detainment does as little damage as possible to the lives and employment possibilities for the one detained. If their permanent employment options get corrupted even though they were wrong, the government can wind up hosting them forever.

A one-day, two-day or week-long stint in a delayed status with communication capability can be a significant low-cost overall realignment of the ability to mediate the cost of the total system in the near term and also the very long time.

The segmented prisoner, defense support teams, could be very useful in determining the practical possibilities to keep the options open and validated before the plea is established. The pause time can allow a cooling off period that can benefit the detained person, and the system and the taxpayers cost considerations.

The support team can also simplify the situation for the detainee's family and reduce stress all around.

12 - Categories of Detainees

The first step for defense support processors is to document information that may be helpful to the counsel for the detainees. There will need to be some standard forms that the court approves that will detail the life and skills or the detainee and their employment and family status.

The overriding principles that are important to dig into are the impact of the detainment on the family to assess the options that will vary by the lifestyle and family dependence on the detainee.

An unemployed single detainee will have all the rights of everyone else. Detainees with a job and a spouse and a child or more could be motivated to help the process along and embrace options.

Pre-plea detention options can make a significant difference in the process of a detainees' judicial experience and the complexity of the steps within that journey. Time is money to the court system but time and information can influence the quality of life for the detainee and their family.

Mental Health Treatment funding and Addiction Treatment funding by employers may be an absolute touchdown for the prisoner defense supporter, and the detainee, and the detainee's family and the system and the taxpayers.

Unemployed single detainees will also benefit from the research and information that is prepared for their counselor and their conversations with prisoner defense supporters can bring peace.

13 - Substance Abuse Detainees

It is not a secret that a lot of the detainees and/or prisoners have issues that may be rooted in substance misuse. When prisoner defense supporters are able to detect through the papers of detainment that a detainee is employed at the time of detainment and has a substance abuse issue, they could initiate an inquiry through the personnel department and or the union of the detainee to find care and accommodation for the detainee that meets their needs.

The society that we all live in is very intense, and everybody can hit a bad patch in the road that knocks them off balance.

People can get physically sick and need to go to the hospital for stabilization and a little rehabilitation.

With the stress of our times, it is also easy for people to become emotionally overwhelmed and do stupid things that cause consequences that need treatment.

Employer Human resources support and union member benefit support are much better options for lesser cases than court rulings and prison records.

In addition to doing right by the detainee, the spouse, children and extended families of the detainees could benefit from not having to endure the emotional and financial costs of having a family member incarcerated.

The saving to our society of having the family self-supported in lieu of state-supported could be significant.

14 - Mental Health Detainees

It is also not a secret that some detainees can have issues that may be rooted in mental illness. When prisoner defense supporters are able to detect through the papers of detainment that a detainee is employed at the time of detainment and may have a mental health concern, they could initiate an inquiry through the personnel department and or the union of the detainee to find diagnosis, care and accommodation for the detainee that meets their needs.

The society that we all live in is very intense, and everybody can hit a bad patch in the road that knocks them off balance.

People can get physically sick and need to go to the hospital for stabilization and a little rehabilitation.

With the stress of our times, it is also easy for people to mentally act out and become emotionally overwhelmed and do stupid things that cause consequences that need treatment.

Employer Human resources support and union member benefit support are much better options for lesser cases than court rulings and prison records.

In addition to doing right by the detainee, the spouse, children and extended families of the detainees could benefit from not having to endure the emotional and financial costs of having a family member incarcerated.

The saving to our society of having the family self-supported in lieu of state-supported could be monumental.

15 - One Day Delay Startup

There are many ways that this could all be organized depending on the flexibility of the court agencies and the prevailing laws in the jurisdiction. It would be my suggestion that a monitored and controlled telephone system be initiated from a segmented prisoner arrangement to a court-controlled temporary holding area.

During the development stage, willing prisoners in segmentation could be encouraged to participate because it is a way to show that they care enough to help the whole system. Of course, legal and appropriate rewards could be incorporated and reasonably expected based on the success of the program for the benefit of the taxpayers and the supervising government agency.

Legal and appropriate rewards are so easy to put down on paper and may not have any real value meaning to the prisoners, but it would be my hope that this program accomplished with integrity could change a lot for a while. It could also quickly evaporate if there were not some early negotiation of values by the participants.

The real benefits for the prisoner defense supporters could be later as they build skills they could take with them into a new career. Another real benefit for the prisoner defense supporter could be some new friends on the outside who could help them with Re-Entry.

The real benefits for society could very well be the quality of life for the children of the detainees who might be saved from the waste of isolation from the loss of the parent they know.

Children with parents in prison may have a much more stressful life, and there have been references in print as to the statistical likelihood of they themselves developing into prisoners.

16 - Diagnostic Evaluations

The diagnostic processes that follow the prisoner defense support inquiries can be valuable to the system whether they result in diverting a detainee or not. Diverting a detainee to an employer-funded treatment facility can save a lot for the prisoner's, prisoner's children, the prisoner's spouse, the legal system, society in general and the taxpayers.

Even if after the delay, the path to prison stays as before for many of the detainees, the diagnostic effort will not be a waste of time as it would determine the definitive needs of the detainee more rapidly than a pro forma evaluation within the system on a routine schedule.

The early information may also help to avert any unanticipated conflicts between persons who have issues that could cause a flare-up between detainees and or prisoners.

At the very least evaluations for Alcohol, Drugs and Mental Illness can provide reference timelines for use later if any of those diagnosed were to have their conditions deteriorate.

The diagnostic evaluations can be a cost-cutting application for the whole system. If any of the detainees are ever saved from incarceration because of the diagnostic assessments, then the entire system wins, the taxpayers get a break, and the lives of the detainees and their families are enhanced.

17 - Cost Savings Could be Tremendous

It would take a lot of investigation to determine average cost savings to the taxpayers of any particular jurisdiction. Cost have reportedly ranged from about $135 to a high of over $400 a day per prisoner. Delay costs may be less but probably no more.

The success of prisoner defense support could be easily justified by the enhancement of the possible enrichments to the jurisprudence system that would include:

1. Proactive assurance that the system costs are being tracked for prudence.

2. Proactive diligence to assure in another way that options are available to avoid unnecessary convictions.

3. Proactive diligence to avoid collateral damage to children who are guilty of nothing.

4. Proactive diligence to avoid collateral damage to spouses and extended family members who are guilty of nothing.

5. Reduced pressure for prosecutors.

6. Increase in the attention and detail assembled pre-plea that can help to destress the detainees' situation so they can avoid making mistakes that could be irreversible.

18 - Quality Of Life Expansion Factors

Many detainees have some family somewhere so we could easily project a much larger group of people can be impacted by being able to justify the deflection and get detainees care in more traditional care systems that are off the expenses that the taxpayers have to pay. The conventional care may cost substantially less, be more efficient and may be covered by some insurance policies or employer programs.

I used the example earlier regarding prisoners indicating that the expansion could be 613% more costly in life disruption than just the costs of incarceration.

My earlier projection used a calculation of spouses, children, mothers, father, and siblings showing that 2.3 million prisoners could directly impact about 14.2 million immediate family members. Of course, that may be a conservative calculation as many prisoners have aunts, uncles, grandmothers, grandfathers, cousins, friends and business associates who will also be impacted.

Collateral Damage Elimination and It's Costs

The possibility of keeping detainees out of prison will also help eliminate the need for some expenses of collateral damage that might occur during incarceration.

19 - Two or More Day Delays

The option to extend delays may prove valuable to all participants in the system. This could be done in the same facility as the One-Day delays, but the criteria and rules would probably need to be separately determined.

This could also be done many ways depending on the flexibility of the court agencies and the prevailing laws in the jurisdiction.

Depending on the options that this program may offer, some candidates may be willing to pay their own way so that they have the opportunity to maximize their options.

This time extension may offer the cost savings of the daily rate, and it may also provide other benefits. It may help with:

1. Visiting can be done between lawyers and detainees without delays or additional taxpayer expense.

2. Employer schmoosing to increase the likelihood of cooperation and support for the detainee.

3. Spouse meetings to support family preparation.

4. Opportunity for meetings with the children of the detainee, so they do not feel they have been abandoned.

5. Progressively advancing options for the court so that cases are well packaged to avoid confusion or review.

6. Family-friendly communications if permitted.

20 - Payback by Saving A Child From Crisis

Regardless of how guilty a prisoner is or how bad they feel about their past, they/you can set out today to help people as an offering to God to help express appreciation for the gifts were given via segmentation.

Paying it forward is something that can be done to show God and the Universe that you care. It may be true that you cannot change the past and what is done is history.

You can change the future history by helping others. Helping a detainee can help that individual, their spouse, their children, their mothers, their fathers, their siblings and many others.

Defense support can reverse the spiral down for one individual at a time and shift the momentum to a spiral up. The good that is shown may not ever get any recognition, but it will be known that enough is changed to change the focus from you to others.

If you believe in God, please know that all is seen, and that is not announced to encourage you into doing something positive. When you are ready to change and put others foremost, the possibility for you to stay in that goal is enhanced.

As you continue to be different, the likelihood of the pattern locking in is enhanced, and the bad in you can be displaced by the good in you.

You have free will, and the things you are disgusted with can be eliminated, and over time, new light can shine on your path and your personal peace. It is always up to you. Think about it.

21 - The Good Defense Support Teams Can Do

Each day is new and fresh, and in it, you have a new block of your lifetime. As you think and vibrate in each day, your energy raises or lowers what will be the resonance of your existence and the vibes that you show to others.

While you have been in prison, it is likely that people and events have contributed to a downward spiral of vibration that is difficult to perceive. The energy of others influences the resonance of the space that they and you have occupied.

The vibration that has circulated is subject to the thought energy of all who occupy the space. As you may have subtly, harmonized with thought energy from others that may not have served you; they also will be influenced by your energy when you choose to direct it consciously.

Like a ripple in a pond from a stone tossed into it, the intensity of vibration has more impact closer to the entry point. Good energy that comes from you now will have an effect on others in the present and the future.

You can create new initiatives that can be referenced in the future as a base of history upon which the detainees and prisoners of the future can be more kindly treated.

22 - Optional Idea
Is Information Shareable with Prosecutors, So the Best Interest of Society is Served?

Prosecutors like Defense Attorneys are officers of the court and may have a variable level of duty to consider some common-sense measures for the efficiency of the proceedings. Care would be needed by the defense support team to avoid introducing information before the plea that could benefit the prosecution.

Prosecutors, however, may benefit from some information that can allow them to see truth efficiently and curtail some perceived but unverifiable concepts that might be costly to the court and unproductive to their professional performance.

After the plea and or after the closure of the case, the information could prove valuable for screening characteristics of detainees lives that may allow prosecutors to serve the community more holistically in the future. Many prosecutors may be elected, and the thoroughness of their public image is important.

Prosecutors may sit at a powerful pivotal place for the integration of information within the community. The defense support team information and the prosecutor's investigative skills may together allow the prosecutors to develop the total experience of detainees in a way that can help them understand and share data about community action to deter crime. That might help the community see the significance of their performance.

23 - Thank You

For
Considering
These
Ideas

24 - Don't Worry Ever

Ever

It Does Not Help Prayer Still Does!

Resource: http://Create-A-Prayer.com

25 - Resource List

Distant Healing Sessions (or Join Mail List) – Write To mikewann@voicenet.com

Books by Rev. Mike at www.Amazon.com:

Veterans Healing Six Pack
1. *Trauma Healing Options for VA Hospitals: Help for Veterans to Own Their Healing and their future.*
2. *Trauma Healing Action Steps for Veterans: Help to Start Healing*
3. *Trauma Healing Action Steps for Veterans: Empowerment*
4. *Trauma Healing Action Steps for Veterans: Forgiveness*
5. *Trauma Healing Action Steps for Veterans: Thought Freedom*
6. *Tea for Veterans: Welcome One Home*

PTSD Power Pack:
1. *The PTSD Project: Turn Pain To Power*
2. *PTSD & Soul Retrieval: Putting One Back Together*
3. *PTSD & The Purple PAD: Calling all Scientists and PTSD Patients*

Angel Raphael Speaks Volume 1: Take Courage! God Has Healing in Store for You!
Angel Raphael Speaks Volume 2: Take Courage! God Has Healing in Store for You!
Angel Raphael Speaks Volume 3: Take Courage! God Has Healing in Store for You!
Angel Raphael Speaks Volume 4: Angels, Addicts, Alcoholics & Prisoners – Oh Yeah!
Angel Raphael Speaks Volume 5: Prisoners Caring for Alcoholics - Australia In Miniature Projects Intro
Angel Raphael Speaks Volume 6: Prisoners Caring for Addicts - Australia In Miniature For Addicts
Reiki Journaling from Japan
Reiki Is Alive: God's Great Gift
Four Parts to Healing
Distant Healing: We Are All Connected

Stress Release Energy Work: How To Cope
Does Reiki Love Heal Cancer?
Group Consciousness
Salute To Philadelphia VA Medical Center: Thank You
Reiki Transcript for Reiki 2 & 3 Channels: Dr. Usui Is That You?
God Bless Kindle & Amazon
Puppies Are Different From People
If Your Dog Dies
Toy Guns Are Obsolete
Great Spirit Made Children With Red Skin: AND
The Cage of Fear: Is Not Locked
God Made Children Red, Yellow, Brown, Black & White: Greet Each Child With Kindness
Emergency Medical Kindness In The Cradle Of Liberty: Big City – Cracked Bell
Angels Are Always Around Addicts and Addicts: Help Is Near Now! Invite It In!
Angels Are Always Around Addicts and Alcoholics: Volume 2 - Tools To Help Re-Light Your Life
Non-Profit Support: Sell Your Story To Support Your Mission
Compliance with Dignity: Give & Get Respect
Don't Worry Ever: It Does Not Help!
Angels and Soul Retrieval:
Prayer Muscle for Addiction

Plus 50+ Prison Books
See Titles http://angelraphaelspeaks.com/prison-books/ or Descriptions at Amazon.com Author Page "Reverend Mike Wanner"

Little Books on Kindle.com by Rev. Mike:
English Medical History Questionnaire For Non-English Speakers
English Language Helper for Non-English Speakers
Wise Wonderful Women Are the Well Of The Family
Answers to Test & Research: Dowsing Power
Crisis? Reiki! Baby? Reiki!
Bible References For Healing
Angel Raphael Speaks – Veterans
The Saint Off Interstate 95

26 - Angels Please Prayers

Addict's
Angels of Healing Selected
Help Me to Stay Directed
Come To Me From The Sky
I Am Ready to Succeed Not Try
If I Don't Invite You In
I Might Not Win
I Have Been Lost For Too Long
Help Me To Stay Strong

&

Alcoholic's
Angels of Healing On High
Help Me to Stay Dry
Come To Me From The Sky
I Am Ready to Succeed Not Try
If I Don't Invite You In
I Might Not Win
I Have Been Lost For Too Long
Help Me To Stay Strong

From

http://AngelRaphaelSpeaks.com/AAAAAAA/

27 - Private Channeling

Angel Raphael Speaks a series of free messages that are channeled through Reverend Mike Wanner for the Highest good and Highest Healing of all concerned.

Many questions arise about Reverend Mike doing private channeling, and he does help with that so e-mail him.

Reverend Mike is available worldwide as a psychic channel, emotional release facilitator, spiritual energy practitioner & teacher, and public speaker. He looks forward to meeting you soon!

Email - <u>mikewann@voicenet.com</u>   215-342-1270

PRIVATE SPIRITUAL READINGS/channelings or Spiritual Healing Sessions: Telephone or in person.

Rev. Mike is available for individual, intuitive one-on-one sessions with you, his Guide Family, and your Guides. He helps by offering clarity on emotional situations about your life, your purpose, your spirituality, and the release of stuffed emotions and cellular memory.

Connect to the love of your Guides today!

Contact Rev. Mike for an appointment.

Sessions available:

Spiritual Readings
Angel Channeling
Distant Reiki Healing
Distant Clearing of Stuffed Emotions
Distant Clearing Cellular Memory
Distant Clearing Energy Blockages
Distant Clearing of the Chakras
Customized needs
Mastermind dowsing responses to yes/no direction finding questions.

Rev. Mike is a facilitator of healing. He brings you and the Divine together so that you can align with the Divine and have a great time and a great life. All healing is between you and God, as it should be.

Go ahead and start without Rev. Mike. Visit his prayer site http://www.Create-A-Prayer.com. Take the first step NOW.

28 - Reverend Mike Wanner

Rev. Mike Wanner started his spiritual and ministerial studies with Reiki in 1993 and had studied seven styles of Reiki in the U.S., Japan, Canada, Denmark and Australia. He is certified to teach. He became certified to teach Integrated Energy Therapy in 1999 and co-taught the first IET class of the new Millennium. Mike began dowsing in 2001.

Ordained as a Metaphysical Minister of the International Metaphysical Ministry and an Interfaith Minister of the Circle of Miracles Ministry, Rev. Mike practices and teaches spiritual energy therapies in the Philadelphia Area.

Rev. Mike holds ministerial degrees from the University of Metaphysics and the University of Sedona. He is a Pastoral Care Associate at Jefferson - Aria - Frankford Hospital. He taught at the National Academy of Massage Therapy and Health Sciences.

Rev. Mike was a faculty member of the Medical Mission Sister's Center for Human Integration's School of Integrated Body/Mind Therapies in Fox Chase, Philadelphia, PA for twelve years.

Rev. Mike is licensed by the teaching of Intuitional Metaphysics to practice Spiritual Healing and Scientific Prayer. Mike is also a Prayer therapist.

Rev. Mike was elected in 2007 to the status of "Fellow of the American Institute of Stress."

In 2008, Rev. Mike became a practitioner of Coincidental Recognition as he incorporated the CoRe system into his spiritual healing practice.

In 2009, Rev. Mike trademarked a new healing process called Quantum Quatro! Subtle Energy System Support®.
In 2011, Rev. Mike joined the outreach program known as the Health Advantage Group.

In 2012, Rev. Mike became a Certified Professional Coach by The Master Coaching Academy and Joined The Personal Empowerment Group.

Prior to his spiritual, ministerial and coaching studies, Rev. Mike worked for Sears Roebuck and Co. while in High School and after graduation, until he joined the U. S. Air Force in 1965. He returned to Sears from Vietnam in 1969 and stayed until 1978. His final Sears assignment was as an efficiency expert in Methods - Operational Research and Development.

He volunteered with Burholme Emergency Medical Services from 1969 and is still a Life Member and Board of Directors Member. He started a private ambulance company in 1975 and worked professionally in the field until 2001 when he devoted his full attention to real estate investing, healing, coaching, and writing.

www.ReverendMikeWanner.com

www.ingramcontent.com/pod-product-compliance
Lightning Source LLC
Chambersburg PA
CBHW030102230526
45471CB00003B/1211